The G

By Sri Swami Satchidananda

Integral Yoga® Publications
Satchidananda Ashram–Yogaville®
108 Yogaville Way, Buckingham
Virginia 23921

www.integralyoga.org

Library of Congress Cataloging in
Publication Data
Satchidananda, Swami.
The Guru Within

I. Title.
2022
ISBN 978-0-932040-06-0

Printed in the United States of America.

Integral Yoga® Publications

"The syllable gu means shadows. The syllable ru, he who disperses them.
Because of the power to disperse darkness, the Guru is thus named."

—*Shukla Yajur Veda, Advayataraka Upanishad* 16

Foreword

Throughout the history of humankind there have always been human beings who felt there must be more to life than what is offered by the physical, emotional, intellectual and socio-political realms alone. Therefore they sought a higher wisdom or spiritual enlightenment.

Many have found themselves in need of someone who has traveled the spiritual path successfully and could guide them toward the understanding they sought.

Thus has the Guru and disciple (or spiritual teacher and student) relationship found a place in nearly every spiritual tradition in the world. There have been enlightened teachers or Gurus since the very dawn of time: Hasidic Rabbis of Judaism, Sufi Masters of Islam, Lord Jesus and the long line of mystics and saints in the Christian tradition. Lord Buddha and all the succeeding Rinpoches, Lamas and Roshis in Buddhism—these are all examples of this important and still living tradition.

Guru-Disciple: A Symbolic Relationship

Since the 1960s, we have seen the influx and influence of many Gurus bringing a variety of teachings to the West and into a culture that was, in many ways, wholly unprepared to understand this. Some students began to blindly follow a Guru, while others when they heard the word "Guru," equated this term with a cult. All of these distortions can happen, not only in the Yoga tradition, but in other traditions, like in the Buddhist tradition, with its own practice of Guru Yoga.

Through venerating a Guru, a lineage and tradition, we are connecting with the principle of *Guru-tattva*. Today, there is a lot of misinformation and misunderstanding about the nature of the Guru. There have also been many problems and abuses that have occurred within this tradition in modern times, with some living teachers. So, we need to be especially clear that the classical principle of *Guru-tattva* does not talk about putting one's complete trust in "a human being," as in the interpersonal level (human being-to- human being). The Guru principle points to the level of transmission—the teachings and practices—coming through this person. And in the Vedic and Yoga traditions, this level stands apart from personality, human foibles, and so on. *Guru-tattva* means the Guru in the role of being a luminous beacon of transmission of a tradition and its teachings.

There are many ways in which we can misunderstand the principle of *Guru-tattva*. For example, this principle can lead us to misunderstand it as some strange type of power dynamic in which we let go of our own inner wisdom and sanity and give that away to some other person, group or organization. This is not a correct understanding of the tradition, which in fact points to—in its fullest sense—helping us get in touch with our inner wisdom.

In the Yoga tradition, the Guru is both a person and is seen as a channel of the teachings, the path and its wisdom—the wisdom we are seeking to wake up to as our essential nature. Ken

McLeod (translator, author, and teacher of Tibetan Buddhism) clarified this in an interview with *Integral Yoga Magazine*, when he said:

"I see a teacher fulfilling three functions: to teach a set of spiritual practices, to show the student what it means to be awake and to point out all the things that get in the way of one's spiritual progress. This is done informally through showing respect and devotion to your teacher. It's done formally through actual practice.

"It's important to understand that this is a form of practice and it is not about taking every single thing the teacher says literally or does as perfect and to be obeyed. In our modern Western society there is the tendency to do just that and it puts the student-teacher relationship at risk.

"Guru Yoga is an advanced practice for this reason, and it is for students whose spiritual practice has reached the level of maturity and the level of maturity in the relationship with the teacher so as to not be confused by the inevitable family-of-origin projections.

"We must have a proper understanding of what our teacher is, namely that aspect of our experience of awakened mind that is showing us how to wake up. This is a symbolic relationship. Is devotion to one's teacher important? Yes. This is how we form a connection with how awakening is manifesting in our own experience, so why wouldn't we be devoted to that? I really don't see how seekers can do this all for themselves."

The classical tradition of the Guru-disciple, or teacher-student, relationship helps us to see, to experience and to fully nurture the quality of wisdom within us. The external teacher—the outer Guru, as opposed to this inner Guru—is really the catalyst that helps us to access this wisdom within ourselves. In fact, there is no other purpose for the outer Guru than to help us to see and experience the inner Guru. *Guru-tattva* is something that has taken time for westerners to even begin to understand in the proper context.

The Importance of Lineage vs. Cultural Appropriation

When we reflect on issues concerning cultural appropriation we want to be very respectful of the Yoga tradition and lineage. How do we do this? By paying respect and honoring the Guru and lineage and by staying true to the teachings of our tradition. In many Yoga, Hindu, Buddhist, and Jain traditions there is a long history of devotion and offerings to the Guru and the lineage. There is an annual day, known as Guru Purnima, during which one's Guru or spiritual teacher is honored.

In Integral Yoga, we observe Guru Purnima annually and we honor our tradition by placing photos of our Guru and his Guru (Swami Satchidananda and Swami Sivananda, respectively) on our altars. Additionally, we honor other faiths and wisdom traditions by placing the Integral Yoga All Faiths Yantra on the altar and photos of the prophets, saints, and sages of many traditions adorn the Satsang Hall at Satchidananda Ashram (and in many of our centers).

We also honor our tradition and lineage by observing the birth anniversaries of Sri Swami Satchidananda and Sri Swami Sivananda. We also annually observe the *Mahasamadhi* anniversary (the day that a realized master has consciously left their body) of our Guru.

Modern yogis may choose to follow their own paths, unassociated with any particular lineage or Guru. And yet, all practitioners of any of the *moksha* traditions have lineage to thank for the existence of Yoga in the current world.

For example, transmission from teacher to student maintaining a direct, unbroken Dharma lineage from the time of the Buddha is one of the cornerstones of Tibetan Buddhism. The blessings of the lineage masters are passed along to the student with the authorization to engage in the practice, creating the auspicious interdependence necessary for authentic accomplishments to ripen.

Integral Yoga, which is a classical Yoga tradition, has direct lineage links from our Guru, Swami Satchidananda to his Guru, Sri Swami

Sivananda; to the Holy Order of Sannyas (of Hindu swamis dating back to the 8th century of Sri Shankaracharya, who formalized the Order); as well as Sri Patanjali (mid-2nd century) who synthesized the *Yoga Sutras*, a foundational Yoga text upon which many of our practices are based (the eight-fold path); and to Swami Satchidananda's root tradition of Tamil Saiva Siddhanta (12–13th centuries).

"The outer Guru appears to tell us about the reality of the Self, who is the inner Guru. With our defective vision we cannot see or experience for ourselves that this is true. It is the outer Guru who tells us, 'Turn within. Put your attention on the inner Guru and let it pull you back into your source.' In addition to giving these instructions, the outer Guru transmits grace to us, cleans our minds, and pushes them towards the inner Guru, the Self. All Gurus are the Self. All Gurus are formless."

—*Sri Ramana Maharshi, 20th century sage*

Devotion to the Guru

One of the most powerful, yet misunderstood, practices of Tibetan Buddhism, Hinduism, and Yoga is Guru Yoga. In classical Yoga, devotion to the Guru is part of the Bhakti Yoga path, one of the main branches of the Yoga tradition.

Bhakti Yoga and Guru Yoga are not about worshipping a Guru as a human being, but rather seeing the Guru as the vehicle through which the wisdom of the tradition is conveyed.

The teachings and practices conveyed enable us to understand, embrace and experience more fully the divine and awakened qualities to which we aspire.

This is the *Guru-tattva* or divine principle we offer our devotion and reverence to as we seek to transform ourselves, integrating these inherent and potent qualities into ourselves. The goal of Bhakti Yoga is to use the emotional energy of devotion to come to this experience.

"When we connect with our heart of devotion, then, in that moment, we are connecting very powerfully, immediately, and directly with the awakened heart of the Guru and the lineage, as well as our own inherently awakened state. Working with our devotion means that we are not just relying on our own efforts. We are opening ourselves to a source of blessings that is an embodiment and a reflection of our own fundamental nature." —*Ponlop Rinpoche, Tibetan Buddhist scholar and meditation master*

"The seekers after liberation should at all times develop Guru-Bhakti because by following the path shown by the Guru, one attains the highest emancipation.... Salutations to Sri Guru who shows the right path to one whose mind is deluded by attachment and thus confused in the forest of *samsara.*"

—*Sri Guru Gita, verses 41& 91, Skanda Purana*

(From the Editors)

Contents

CHAPTER 1
What is a Guru?

The term "Guru" seems to be very much misunderstood and sometimes misused in this country. The literal meaning of Guru is "teacher." But normally the word is used for a spiritual teacher, one who helps you in realizing your own Spirit by removing the ignorance which veils it.

The word "Guru" is made up of two syllables: "gu" and "ru." "Gu" means the darkness of ignorance, "ru," the one who dispels. So the one who dispels your ignorance is "Guru." In our ordinary life, if somebody teaches you a little bit of cooking, he or she is your guru; a little of your ignorance regarding cooking is removed. But our spiritual Guru is the one who removes the basic ignorance, the ignorance of the true Self.

Sometimes I say, "Knowing no thing brings nothing, knowing everything brings something, but knowing the Knower brings everything." It may sound a little tricky but if you think about it for a moment you will probably get it. Knowing no thing brings nothing—that part is obvious. Knowing everything brings something—something is better than nothing, no doubt. But know the Knower and you will get everything. As the Bible says, "Seek ye first the Kingdom of Heaven and everything else will be added unto thee."

In other words you don't have to grab the knowledge of things one by one. Just grasp the main root and you will get the whole tree. What is the cause of all our many doubts, fears, anxieties and little ignorances? The basic ignorance of our own Self (essence-nature). Know the Self and you will know what is to be known. So the one who helps you in removing that self-ignorance is called the Guru.

CHAPTER 2
Is a Guru Necessary?

What is the necessity for a Guru or spiritual master?

At least to answer such questions! Actually that is the duty of a teacher—and their purpose. You may call them "Master" because they seem to know what they are talking about. As you know, the Sanskrit term for the spiritual master is "Guru"—the one who eliminates or removes the darkness in your understanding.

You ask me, "What is the necessity?" You feel the necessity for a guide only when you do not know your way. If you know already, there's no need for a Guru.

But even in the worldly sense we always seem to understand things through the help of somebody. When you come into the world as a baby, the mother acts as your guru.

The Hindu scriptures say that everyone should have four Gurus: *Mata, Pita,* Guru, *Deva. Mata:* the mother. *Pita:* the father. Guru: the spiritual guide.

And, ultimately, *Deva*: God. The parents take you to the Guru and the Guru takes you to God.

Even in our normal life we take the help of many gurus. When such is the case even in the normal worldly life, how could it be otherwise in the spiritual life? Your spiritual Guru is even more necessary than the worldly ones, because the spiritual life is much more subtle.

Many people read a lot of books about Yoga and spiritual life, but books alone can never take the place of a Guru. If we could learn everything through books there should be only publishing houses and no universities.

Books cannot take the place of a teacher because when you read a book, you can learn from the book but the book can never teach you. You should know the difference. It is up to you to correctly understand what you read.

The author might even have given the right meaning with all good intentions, but you read it any way you want because you are trying to understand it with the help of your own mind, your own understanding. The entire responsibility lies in your hands. You can understand or misunderstand. That is why we see quite a lot of misinterpretations even in the spiritual field.

People read the books and then just understand or interpret as they want and even teach others that their interpretation is what Yoga is. But a Guru will not allow you to misunderstand.

The moment they feel you have not understood something correctly they will say, "Hey, that's not right; this is the way." A book will not and cannot do that. That's why you need a person who has gone through the path and realized the goal to guide you in what is to be done. So I would say a spiritual teacher is very necessary.

CHAPTER 3
Qualities of a Guru

What are the qualities of a Guru? How can you recognize a Guru?

That is a very beautiful question. In fact in the *Bhagavad Gita*, Arjuna (the disciple) asks Lord Krishna (the Guru) the very same question, though using a slightly different word instead of Guru. He says:

"What, O Krishna, is the description of one who has steady wisdom and is merged in the superconscious state? How do they speak, how do they sit, how do they walk?" (Chapter II, *sloka* 54)

A Guru is the one who has steady wisdom, a "*stithapragnyam*" in Sanskrit: one who has realized the Self. Having that realization, you become so steady; you are never nervous. You will always be tranquil, nothing can shake you. Your *pragnyam*, or knowledge, never fades nor gets clouded over. It is always in the Light. You call such a person an enlightened person, "*stithapragnyam*," a person of steady wisdom.

Now, how would you know them? It is very difficult because we all look more or less the same, is it not? We all have heads, shoulders, hands, trunk, legs. A person is a person, after all. That's why we sometimes hear, "What is this Guru business?

A Guru is just a person like us." Yes, physically. When you see with the physical eye you see the physical body and that body is in no way different from yours. Sometimes the Guru's body may even be weaker or more sickly than yours. Is that body the Guru then? Then how can we recognize the Guru?

Lord Krishna answers:

"One whose mind is not perturbed by adversity, who does not crave for pleasure, who is free from attachment, fear and anger, is the sage of steady wisdom." (Ch. II, 56)

"One who is unattached everywhere, who is neither delighted at receiving good or dejected by evil, is poised in wisdom." (II, 57)

Such a person is what you call a Guru. It is not the body or the mind or the intellectual understanding—it is the Self that you call Guru. Only in the Self can there be perfect equanimity. It is that Divine within, not the person, remember that. A person can never have this. When you see somebody and say "Guru" you don't mean the physical body or their intelligence, you mean the Self.

That Self is in everything, in everybody, so the Guru is also in everything. In reality every one of you is a Guru. But the trouble is that some people seem to know it, many do not seem to. We were all born with that knowledge but somehow we seem to have lost it. We call this "growing up."

But certainly we know that an undesirable "growth" has to be operated on and removed, is it not? And that is the business of the one whom you call a Guru. Sometimes they perform gentle operations, sometimes really difficult ones, sometimes with a little local anesthesia, sometimes with total anesthesia.

"One attains peace in whom all desires enter as waters flow into the ocean, which filled from all sides remains unmoved; but not one who is full of desires." (II, 70)

That steady-minded person is like the ocean—totally contented. They are a person above wants.

What is meant by "a person above wants?" They have no wants; they never want anything. And because they don't want anything, it seems that all the things which are normally wanted by others want them. Isn't it funny?

That's why the example of the ocean is given. The ocean never wants anything. It never sends invitations to all the rivers: "Hey, Missouri, come and meet me; Ganges, come; Kaveri, come; Mississippi, come."

The ocean is just there and so all the rivers say, "Hey, I want to fall into you, I am falling in love with you." They really do fall in love with the sea and run headlong toward it like a mad lover running toward the beloved.

And what happens to the rivers when they reach the ocean? Before they arrive, they seem to have their own distinctions. Each has a different name, sometimes even a different color, size, shape, everything.

But once they fall into the sea—into the arms of their beloved—they seem to lose all their distinctions.

And another important point is this: imagine that you don't want anything; you are just contented. So then everything starts coming to you. What will happen? Gradually your ego might begin to swell up, is it not?

But in the case of the sea it doesn't happen. Even after everything comes to it, it knows its own proper limit; it never swells up. So the sea teaches us these two qualities of a *stithapragnyam*.

And this would also let you know what would be the Guru's attitude toward their disciples. Would a Guru make disciples? Not at all. No Guru is interested in creating disciples. Let us know that.

In fact no Guru will even declare themselves a Guru. It is the disciples who recognize that person as the Guru. They make them a Guru. If there are no disciples, how can they call themselves a Guru?

It is because a disciple learns something from someone that they call them a teacher. Otherwise they are just there. "Ask, it shall be given," the Bible says. Knowing the fitness of the student and their desire to receive, the Guru gives to them. Otherwise the Guru waits.

And this would also tell you that the Guru will not go after preaching. They are not a missionary. They won't knock on your door and say, "Come on, read this. If you reject it you will go to Hell."

Maybe just to make it a little easier to find them, they will say, "I am here." If you see something special and think they can help you, you go to them. Then they will reveal themselves.

So when a person really gets tired of the worldly pursuits and feels they are not finding any eternal, everlasting peace and happiness, they come looking for peace and joy. Then the Guru helps them.

And how will a person of steady wisdom look at things? In the 18th *sloka* of the fifth chapter, Lord Krishna says,

"Those of Self-knowledge look with equal vision on a *brahmana* [a spiritual person] imbued with learning and humility, a cow, an elephant, a dog and an so-called 'outcaste.'" (V, 18)

In other words they will not make distinctions. They will be totally impartial. Whether they see a sinner or saint, their eye is totally neutral—like the sun. The sun shines not only on a palace but even on a dilapidated hut or a deserted beach.

You see that equanimity everywhere in nature. A rose will smell the same whether you have bought it, borrowed it or even stolen it. It will not say, "No, no, no, you didn't buy me. You stole me from the garden. I won't give you the smell."

It is only the human beings who see with these distinctions: language, skin color, caste, country. Nature has "*samadarshinam*"—equal vision. And that is also the quality of a steady-minded person.

Lord Krishna speaks more about the qualities of an enlightened person in the twelfth chapter. But here he uses a different name for the person of steady wisdom. He calls them "a true devotee," one who is very dear to the Lord.

Arjuna asks Krishna, "Which kind of devotee is really dear to You? You seem to be calling everybody Your dear, but who is really Your very, very most beloved?

Krishna answers: "One who hates no being, who is friendly and compassionate to all, who is free from the feeling of "I" and "mine," equal-minded in pain and pleasure and forgiving;" (XII, 13)

"Ever-contented, steady in meditation, self-controlled and possessed of firm conviction, with mind and intellect dedicated to Me. My devotee, is dear to Me." (XII, 14)

"He by whom the world Is not agitated and whom the world cannot agitate; who is free from joy, envy, fear and anxiety, is dear to Me." (XII, 15)

You might wonder what "free from joy" means. It doesn't mean they are always morose. You could say they don't get excited. Because if they got excited, naturally the opposite should happen—they should get depressed.

So they get neither excited nor depressed. They remain centered, because they have a constant excitement within. There's nothing more exciting than that for them. They see everything outside as just temporary, just normal, and just fun.

They are always in that intoxication from within, so nothing else can intoxicate them anymore. My Guru, Swami Sivanandaji used to sing: "*Hara halume alumastu satchidananda hum*: At all times I am Existence, Knowledge, Bliss Absolute!"

You can all say that because you are all that *satchidananda* (existence-knowledge-bliss). In truth, you are that Guru—you are that Self. And once you realize that, you will be possessed by all these beautiful qualities. Nothing will be able to shake you.

And until that happens, nothing else can save you. So let us realize that Self first. Lord Krishna goes on:

"One who neither rejoices nor hates nor grieves nor desires, renouncing good and evil, who is full of devotion; that one is dear to Me." (XII, 18)

"One who is the same to foe and friend, in honor and dishonor; who is the same in cold and heat, in pleasure and pain, who is free from attachment." (XII, 18)

It means they are totally balanced. If someone brings me a beautiful garland of roses, you might say, "Oh, you should have seen the Swami's face. He was so happy about it." But if somebody had made a beautiful garland out of worn out shoes, I should still smile the same way.

Imagine if somebody praises: "Oh, you are a wonderful man. You did this and that; oh, you are a great Guru with so many thousands of disciples." Then, all of a sudden, from a corner we hear: "Bogus fellow, how many of you are running around this country? You couldn't do anything in your own country so you came here, huh? Rogue!" You should still smile at them. Think, "That's the way they see me. They have the feeling to see me that way. Why should I worry about it?"

You know what you think about you. If you accept what he says, it means you don't know who you are. Somebody else has to tell you who you are.

If one person says you are great and you get excited, and another says you are terrible and you feel depressed, that means you don't know who you are. If you're a monkey and someone says you're a donkey, would you be worrying over it? No. "Well, probably you have a donkey's eye to see a monkey as a donkey, sir." That's what.

So don't try to look for credit or praise from others. If you know who you are, you don't need to worry about others' opinions. Nothing affects you—pleasure or pain, praise or censure. That is the sign of a person of steady wisdom, or a true devotee of God, or a Guru.

All of this is not just something intellectual. It's not that such a person makes a mental adjustment or alignment. If that were so it would be liable to get misaligned also. If a car runs on a bumpy road, the alignment may go wrong and have to be aligned again and again. So this is not mere intellectual understanding, let us know that. We can first know the Self intellectually, but we should ultimately experience it. And the experience comes only when we know who we are without the slightest doubt.

Again and again I would like to remind you not to take the physical body or even the intelligence of a teacher as the Guru. It is the Self. Because they have realized their Self or essence-nature, their intelligence gets a clearer light and their realization reflects through their intelligence.

Then that intelligence talks of something because of that experience, not because their intelligence alone is something special. So when you address somebody as the Guru you are addressing the Self. Let us know that positively.

The scriptures say, "*Guru Shivo, Guru Devo, Guru Bandhu, Guru Sariram. Guru Atma, Guru Jivo, Guroranyam Na Vidyate*. Guru is Lord Shiva; the Guru is Divine; the Guru is your friend; Guru is your body; Guru is your Self; Guru is your soul and there is nothing but the Guru."

That means ultimately everything is that Self. With a description like this, who is not the Guru then? Can I say, "I am the Guru; you are not?" No, everybody is the Guru. But when you do not seem to know that, you just ask me and I say, "You are that." This is the final instruction the Guru can give a disciple when they are fit to understand it— simply "You are That."

But unfortunately if we just say that people think, "Is it that simple? Shouldn't it be something really difficult and complicated?" Our intelligence and ego wants something complicated.

Many people ask me, "What is your technique?" I say, "Be good, do good, be a nice person and lead a selfless life. Take care of your body and take care of your mind." "Is that all? Is that what you call Integral Yoga? I thought you had some special technique?"

So then probably to satisfy their curiosity we have to have something more. But the truth is, "Blessed are the pure in heart; they shall see God." Simple. Just become pure physically and mentally. You will see God. Then you won't need me anymore.

"But won't you show God to us?" I'm not here to show you God. Nobody can ever show God to you. If the Guru does anything, they help you remove the curtain that veils you from recognizing your own Divinity. Then you can see it. That is what is meant by Guru.

CHAPTER 4

Gurus and Spiritual Experiences

Swamiji, what about Gurus like Sri Ramakrishna Paramahamsa? We read that he touched his disciple Swami Vivekananda and Vivekananda had a spiritual experience. Was Vivekananda just opening up something from within himself or did Sri Ramakrishna really transmit something?

Yes, he did transmit something. But if you read further in the same story, Vivekanandaji could not retain the experience. Sri Ramakrishna just gave him a little nibble. Then he said, "Don't depend on my touch every time. Now you know there is something beyond; work it out yourself." Then it took many years for Vivekanandaji to get that experience again.

Sri Ramakrishna gave even that little experience to him because Vivekananda was fit for it. Still, he said, "This is borrowed. I'm giving you a sample." It's something like if I am eating some nice candy and you come along and say,

"Hey, what is that?" "Candy." "Ah, can I try some?" "Okay, a little piece." "Ah, it's so nice. Where can I get some more?" "Go, work, earn money, go to the shop and buy it." I just gave you a taste; then you have to work for it.

Sri Ramakrishna had several thousand disciples but he didn't give all of them even that little taste Vivekanandaji got. So the student should have the proper qualifications for such an experience.

Otherwise, if it is just that easy, Ramakrishna could have just touched everybody and said, "Come on, everybody is a Ramakrishna now." He was not really stingy. He could have done that to a thousand people. Why should he do it to only one, Vivekanandaji? That is the proof that there are certain qualifications necessary even to perceive something like that.

The scriptures say that there are three aids to realize the Truth: the scriptures themselves, the Guru and your spiritual practice. The scriptures tell you that sugar is sweet. The Guru will show you that sugar. Your practice will give you the taste.

The Guru will not put the sugar in their mouth and say, "It is very sweet." You have to taste it yourself. Even if you open your mouth and they put the sugar in, if your tongue is totally coated, you can't taste it. It will be bitter to you. So you have to clean your tastebuds. That is the reason we say the disciple must be fit to know the taste.

How many people were able to perceive Jesus Christ when he ascended? Only the very few who really had that faith and devotion. So it needs a lot of sincerity, purity of heart and devotion to get a little glimpse. And even then, that just becomes a kind of small incentive to work with.

Chapter 5
Qualifications of a Disciple

What are the qualifications of a disciple? How should one approach the Guru?

They should have the sincerity and acknowledge that they know nothing—in the spiritual sense. They should not say, "I do know something, but can you add a little more?'

When Arjuna was standing on his chariot in the midst of the battlefield, he argued with Lord Krishna about what he should do because his mind was deluded by his emotions.

He didn't want to do his duty and fight, so he brought all kinds of philosophical arguments to support his position. But ultimately he realized his foolishness and said,

"My nature is weighted down with the taint of feeblemindedness. My understanding is confused as to my duty. I entreat You to say definitely what is good for me. I am Your disciple. Do instruct me who has taken refuge in You." (II, 7)

That is what you call total surrender. You accept your ignorance. Then you are totally free from that egoism. You come with a clean vessel. As long as the ego is in charge of the vessel, whatever the Guru might put in would get contaminated.

This reminds me of a Zen story. A disciple went to a Master asking him for some wisdom. The Master said, "Okay, I'll give you the wisdom, but first have a cup of tea with me." He began to pour the tea into the disciple's cup. He went on pouring and pouring until the cup was flowing over. Still he kept on pouring.

The disciple said, "Sir, it's already full and you're still pouring. The tea is going on the ground, not into the cup." "Oh, I see. Well, it is the same with your mind. It's already full. Whatever I say is going to overflow your cup; it can't go in. You'd better go empty your 'cup' and then come back."

A seeker after enlightenment should say, "I'm just empty, hollow. You are holy. Please pour that holiness into this hollowness. I am a "holey" reed, please play your music through me." Think of the beautiful flute. It's nothing but a reed full of holes. It doesn't have anything inside and therefore whatever the flutist wants to play, they can. A student should be like that. You simply say, "I'm ready to follow."

Here I'm talking about the attitude of the disciple. But of course the Guru should not simply say, "Do it." Sometimes they may have to do that to test the quality of your mind, your obedience, your egolessness. But normally they will always try to convince you. That is the responsibility of the Guru.

But when it is a question of the attitude of the disciple, this is it. That is the reason I say you can easily find lots of Gurus, but it is rather hard to find one good disciple. It's easy to teach but hard to learn. Lord Krishna also says about discipleship:

"Seek that enlightenment by prostrating, by questions and by service. The wise seers of that Truth will instruct you in that Knowledge." (IV, 34)

Fall at the Guru's feet. It's not to glorify them— you don't need to do that because they are already glorified in their own Self-Realization. It doesn't matter to them whether you fall at their feet or jump on their shoulders. Who is it that benefits when you prostrate? You do. You show that you are humble and egoless; it takes a lot of courage to do that.

And you can't receive without being humble. The giving hand is always above and the receiving hand underneath. That's why you bow down. Otherwise, you won't receive that much. You may simply go to a Guru and treat them as an equal. You exchange your ideas. "These are my beliefs, what about yours?" If they say something, you say, "Oh, I see. I don't seem to agree with you. Goodbye." And you go.

You are simply exchanging ideas, you are not learning. If you want to learn from the Guru, go with an empty heart. Let them fill you with what they have. Don't go to test whether they say what you think. Then you are simply there to check, like you would go to a library.

To be a good disciple means you should first tell the Guru, "I don't know anything. I trust you completely. Tell me what to do and I'm ready to do it." It's only then that the real Guru-disciple relationship begins. Until then, it's just a kind of friendly exchange .

Then put your questions to them: "Where am I? What am I? Why am I? What am I to do?" Question them with sincerity—not to test their capability. Let them know you really want to learn by questioning them. Then third, serve them. You should not get anything without giving everything you can. So these three are the qualifications of a disciple.

CHAPTER 6
How to Receive from a Guru

How can we be most receptive to a Guru's teaching?

All right, so now you have a Guru. You've come across somebody who is ready to teach you and who says they have gone the path—they know something—and are willing to teach you. But you still can't learn unless you have the proper attitude to receive their teaching. A Guru will not force anything into you. They will wait until you ask for it, until you become ready.

This is where the devotion, the *bhakti*, comes in. Unless you have faith you can't receive what they have to give you. Devotion means you put the entire faith in them. That faith becomes your connecting link.

Once that trust is established, even if the Guru refuses to teach you, you will learn from them because the power of faith is that much. By your own faith you will be able to understand what they have in their mind; they need not even tell you.

Without their even opening their mouth you can understand them, because you have established the true communication.

The real teaching, or imparting of the true knowledge, is not normally done with words. We should always remember that. A Guru many give hours and hours of lectures, but it will be just nothing compared with one minute of silent imparting. Words have their limitations, but in silence—by speaking through silence—in the proper communication, in feeling, you receive much more.

It is impossible to put everything in words. In fact, the true feelings should not even be expressed because you will limit them with your words. I see couples, mainly in the West, saying, "Honey, I love you; Honey I love you." They waste their words and their energy. If your beloved tells you "I love you" a hundred times a day, please know for certain they are not loving you. They themself are doubtful about it and that's why they're telling you again and again. If love is truly there, why should they have to tell you? You could feel it. Love is not in words. It is something beyond words. The very look, the very closeness, their every action will be filled with that. So it is a matter of feeling, not hearing.

The relationship between Guru and disciple is the same way, without words they can communicate. But that needs the proper relationship, the proper devotion. Why does the child understand the mother? Because she loves them so much and they reciprocate. Even if the mother is far away, she can easily feel when her baby is hungry. Even though she is working in the office and the baby is at home, a true mother can exactly say, "Oh, my baby is hungry now. I have to go feed them." The baby need not telephone—the feeling comes in the heart.

I have seen this with my own eyes out in the Indian countryside with the farm workers. The mother will be working in the fields and the child will be sleeping in a small hammock under the branch of a tree a half mile away. The mother can't even hear the cry of the baby. All of a sudden she will drop everything, "Oh, my baby is hungry; I must go feed them." If you go with her you can actually see the baby crying there. Out of curiosity I even asked one mother, "How do you feel that? Do you hear the baby crying?" "No, Swami. I get a feeling, there is a kind of sensation, that the baby is waiting for the milk." There are no words; you can't put it into any test tube.

In the same way, true devotion creates that feeling. The Guru knows what the disciple needs and the disciple knows what the Guru wants to communicate—all without words.

Chapter 7
Devotion to a Guru

What is Guru bhakti and how is it to be practiced?

Devotion to the Guru is called *Guru bhakti*. But that is a very high form of *bhakti*. It is the highest one, I would say, because it is very difficult. Anything that is very difficult should be supreme.

God is supreme because God is so difficult to realize; if you could easily see God everywhere, you would probably just say, "I'll take care of You later on. Wait while I finish my card game and then I'll come to You." As the saying goes, 'Familiarity breeds contempt."

So the devotion shown to one's own Guru is really difficult and that is why it is supreme. Why do I say it is difficult? Because you constantly have to prove yourself to be a true disciple. You can easily act like a true disciple in front of a statue or a photo. You can go with some offering, put it there, kneel and pray while your mind is wandering around in a bar or cinema.

You may stand in front of the altar and say, "Oh, God in the Heaven, I am Thine, all is Thine, Thy will be done," and the statue will just be standing there watching you. It won't say, "Hey, what are you doing? Are you praying or looking at the girl next to you?"

A Guru will immediately question you. You can even sit in front of a deity in the name of meditation and fall asleep. The symbol or picture on the altar will just be there; they won't pull your hair and say, "Hey, what are you doing? Shape up! Either sit and meditate properly or go out and do something else."

But if you sit in front of a Guru and meditate, they will keep an eye on you. They may also appear to be meditating, but they will be meditating on you. You meditate on them and they meditate on you. So you have to prove yourself to be sincere—you can't escape from that.

Another thing is that the statue is always the same; there's never any change in it. Whenever you come you see the same statue. It is more or less eternal—it's always God to you. But it's not so in the case of the Guru. One day they will appear to be the great teacher, the great Master, the Self-Realized soul. The next day they will be like an ordinary person. On the third day they will appear a bit crazy and the fourth day like some person shouting at you. Can they be a Guru?"

Or sometimes they will ask you to get up at four or five a.m. for meditation, but when you knock at their door they might be sleeping even at eight o'clock. "My goodness! What is this Guru business then?"

So it is very difficult to have devotion to your Guru because you see their human side. They are still a human being—otherwise They wouldn't be there in your midst. They have a human body; they behave like a human being in many ways.

People think if someone is a Guru they will always be flying in the air. No, they have their body and mind. You don't always see the divine aspects. Sometimes they might even look like a devil or a crazy mad person. They are a mixture of everything.

Also, the Guru won't always conform to your expectations of them. You may have your own imagination about how a Guru should be. Sometimes what we read in books seems to be something different. At least in the ancient books they always have the Guru sitting in lotus posture with eyes closed in *samadhi*.

And particularly in the case of a monk or *sannyasi*, they should embrace poverty. They should have just an old broken clay bowl to eat from, some rags to wear. They won't even have a comb, so their hair will be all matted. They will be sleeping in a small hut somewhere. See?

Each one has their own imagination about the Guru. Some may say, "If he's a yogi, why should his beard be turning white? Can't he stop it?" People even ask that. "Do you sleep? Do you use pillows?

I remember in the 1960s, people would ask, "Do you sleep on a bed of nails?" So it's not possible to live up to your expectations. That is the problem with devotion to the Guru. Because *Guru bhakti* is very difficult, it is placed above all the other forms of worship. According to the Hindu tradition there are six ways of worshipping the Absolute through different names and forms.

If you worship Shiva (Shiva means auspicious), you are called a Shaivite. If you worship Vishnu (Vishnu means omnipresent), you are a Vaishnavite. If you worship God as all-powerful, as the Goddess Parashakti, you are called a Shakta. Others worship God as all-intelligence, in the form of the elephant-headed Lord Ganesh, so they are called Ganapatyam.

And still another group worships God as Kumar, Subramanya or Muruga—the ever-young and beautiful. And the last group says, "These others are all somehow connected with human forms. Instead let us worship God as the Light. The light we can see every day is the sun. So let's worship God as the sun." And they are called Sauravas. These are the six traditional forms of Hindu worship.

But Guru worship is called "transcending the six." Why? Because it is the most difficult. Shiva is always Shiva for you. Vishnu is always Vishnu. If you go in front of Vishnu and sing "*Om Namo Narayana, Om Namo Narayana*" and fall asleep, Narayana (Vishnu) is not going to come and pinch you.

But if you do that in front of a Guru they will question, "What are you doing? Meditating or sleeping?" And if you go in front of a deity's picture, you can offer anything you want—sometimes ripe bananas, sometimes rotten bananas. The deity never questions you about that. But the Guru will question you.

It is rather difficult to please the Guru. They're not always lovable and sweet to you. Sometimes you may even feel, "What destiny brought me to this crazy person?" You will feel like jumping out of the fire.

The Guru is a cook, but sometimes you may think they are a crook! When they really test you a lot you may think, "Are they mad? They can't be Divine; they don't even seem to care about me! My mother and father never treated me like this.

None of my friends would treat me like this. Who is this person? Why am I here?"

But if you are wise, you will realize, "Oh no, if I jump out, I won't get well cooked." When the fritter is put in the boiling oil, it is put in to get fried. However much noise it makes it has to stay in the oil.

Until you are well-roasted, the Guru will keep the lid down on the pot. They will say, "Don't come out. Wait." With all that, if you jump out what will happen? You will land in the fire. If you want yourself to be useful to humanity, you should get yourself well-cooked so all your selfishness is removed.

There are so many incidents to disturb your faith. But with all that if you say, "Well, I don't know. They must have a purpose behind it. They are my Guru. I have full trust, implicit faith in them. I'm not here to question or judge them, I'm here to be trained by them," that is true devotion. You have to allow yourself to be in their hands. Some people don't have the patience. They think the Guru should always pamper them and say, "Oh, you are brilliant, beautiful. Hey, everybody, look at my disciple!" They may even say that sometimes, but then if they see your ego swelling a little bit, they'll say, "Hey stop that!"

One time they'll praise you, then immediately they will crush your ego. It's necessary. They had to go through all this before with their teacher.

But it's not that easy. That is why people keep on changing teachers. If they are very nice to you, you say, "Oh, they are my wonderful Guru; they love me so much. They are always nice to me. . ." But, what happens if they don't look at you for a few days: "I must think of which other Guru will be more loving and kind to me."

So the Guru is at you constantly and very often your faith is shaken. But if you are going to keep on with the same faith even in the face of all these obstacles, why can't we say *Guru bhakti* is the highest form of devotion? If anyone has that faith, they are really fortunate. They are probably even better than the Guru. They are fit to receive everything because of their faith. They can learn more from the Guru than even the Guru knows because their faith itself acts as their Guru then. Real faith is God after all. That's why the Bible says if you have even the faith the size of a mustard seed, you can move mountains. But if that is shaken, even with the most wise of all the Gurus, you won't receive anything because there is no communication.

Faith is the greatest virtue and doubt the worst thing. Remember that. If a little doubt gets into your life, the entire life is poisoned. On the other hand, with just a little faith, the entire life will grow beautifully.

But in this modern age we say, "Oh, how can I have faith in the Guru unless I know for certain what they are? You can't know and you can't judge intellectually, but you can feel. The heart is the same with everybody, so go according to your feeling. Use your intelligence but don't always rely on that. Intelligence has its limitations, but if it works together with the heart it will be really wonderful.

CHAPTER 8

How to Choose a Guru

I've heard that one must not accept someone as their Guru unless they have tested them. How can you do that?

It is very difficult to understand a Guru just by your intelligence. Beyond that something will tell you—you will get a kind of feeling: "I think they are my Guru." You have to follow how you feel about them. Your heart should tell you, "Yes, so-and-so can guide me on the path."

Or, you can use your intelligence and question the Guru's students. "How are they? Have they really taught you something?" When you go to a shop to buy fruit, how can you know if it will be really sweet? The shopkeeper knows for certain that it's good.

But if you don't want to believe them, you can ask your friends, "Have you tried any of the fruit from this shop?" "Oh, yes, I bought some yesterday. It's really very sweet." Then you believe your friend and take some. So ask a few friends.

See whether that teacher is really useful to many people, whether there are many people who follow their advice and are benefited.

Still another way is to see if they practice what they preach. They may be talking of Yoga and how Yoga is all serenity and keeping a peaceful mind, how you should never get upset over anything.But spy on them for some time and see whether they get upset over anything.

Any swami or yogi will say, "Keep calm always; don't get upset over anything." But you have to see whether they express that in their very life. You can even test them. Go to them and say, "I've seen hundreds of imposters like you calling themselves "Gurus." I don't believe you are authentic and don't want you." See how they react.

But you should also know that it's very difficult to test a Guru. Sometimes they may even act like they are getting upset over something but they will be just using their anger to teach someone a lesson. So if you want to test them like that, you should be sure of your capacity to understand their reactions.

One thing I would like to say, if you are really interested in finding a Guru, your own keen interest will show you the way. You don't need to worry about it. If you can't decide, say "Alright, I will follow your teachings for some time, one or two or three months. If nothing happens, that's it. If I get a little taste, then I'll know there's something there and I'll take a little more."

It's much better to do that than to just trust anyone immediately if you're not sure. I have seen many people coming and saying, "Oh, you are my all, you are everything; I give myself totally to you." Then within a few weeks they are saying, "Oh, I've seen hundreds like them." So it is best neither to take it on too quickly, nor to just drop it and go away very soon. Have the proper distance, see how you feel, and then come close gradually.

CHAPTER 9

Mantra Meditation without a Guru

Can one do mantra meditation without a Guru?

Sure you can. But what we call mantra initiation is not just giving you a mantra or telling you what to repeat. The person who gives you initiation will impart a little of that mantra vibration into you. It's like putting a drop of yogurt culture into a big pot of milk, the milk becomes solidified quickly. Without that culture it might take more time for the milk to ferment and curdle by itself. And probably then it will be a little sour too!

So it is to get that drop of beautiful culture that you take initiation from a Guru. But you don't need to wait for that. You can just repeat any mantra, there's nothing wrong with it. Nobody would say, "Without a Guru you cannot practice anything." Actually, your own intuition can be your Guru. You can get guidance from within.

It's only if you can't get that inner guidance that you seek guidance from outside. Ultimately, you are the Guru. Why do I say this? Because if your inner knowing is not going to be your Guru, you won't even be able to recognize a Guru outside. It is your inner knowing that tells you, "Oh, so-and-so seems to be a nice guide, follow them." You listen to that first and then follow a person according to that intuitive sense.

Your mind might say, "Oh, there are so many fakes running around, why worry about all those people?" What will you do? You won't be able to see any Guru outside then. So a good mind and an intuitive sense will guide you to a good person.

CHAPTER 10
The Guru Within

Please speak on feeling the Guru within.

There is a Guru within you. Guru is not a "person." Guru is the omnipresent Consciousness that pervades everywhere, that guides the entire universe constantly. This is what is meant by *Guru-tattva*, the Guru principle.

Guru-tattva is that self-illuminating power of Consciousness that manifests as all that teaches us. But because the Guru is within you, and you have never seen or experienced it, you need a reflection to help you recognize it. The Guru holds up the mirror showing you that. The external Guru is to point out the Guru within you.

The conscience within you is the Guru. The one that guides you. The one that enlightens you. As such, there is a Guru in everybody. The external Guru and the teachings are to guide you to go within and recognize that Guru within who is constantly guiding us. It is there the external

Guru comes. With the help of the teaching, you will realize your own Guru within. As I said before, the Guru is the one who removes your darkness—somebody who throws light on your life, on your doubts. But removing darkness doesn't mean you take a knife and scrape it off or take a stick and beat it out.

How can you remove darkness? Can you come and shout, "Hey, darkness, get out!"? No. You just quietly bring in a light and the darkness goes away. So the one who shines a light, the one who helps you recognize the enlightenment, the truth of your essence-nature is the Guru.

The Guru helps you to recognize that there is something—and there always was something—in you that seems to know what is happening in you, is it not? This knower is what we call "Awareness" or "Consciousness." That is the same in essence as the Cosmic Consciousness. And this Consciousness or knowing is common to us all; it is a constant in our lives. You never stop knowing. You are always a knower. There is no doubt about it, is there? And that knowing, is the pure Consciousness or the Light in you.

So as the person who knows everything, you are the Light, you are the Guru. Apply that knowledge to the things you do not know and that is using the Guru within.

If you don't know how to apply your own inner knowing, then you go to somebody who has that capacity. You say, "Hey, how do you seem to know?" They will ask you, "What makes you think you don't know also?" See? They just help you know yourself as that pure Consciousness, the Knower of everything. You just take the help of somebody who has achieved that knowledge to help you know it too.

That is the job of the Guru. Otherwise, you would be depending on an outside Guru always. Then they are not really helping you; they are probably making some business out of you or making you dependent on them for some reason. Whenever and wherever possible they should point out that you have it all within yourself already. It's like the example of someone who buys a new piece of gold jewelry—a necklace or gold chain. They put on the jewelry and then forget about it. All of a sudden they remember, "Hey, I bought some new jewelry, but I don't remember where I put it." They run around searching for it in a panic. "Where is my necklace?" they wonder. The jewelry is around their neck but they can't see it! All of a sudden they come across a mirror. "Ah, there it is!" Then they stop running around and searching because they know they have it on.

The Guru's duty is just to show you that you have that gold piece already—the golden peace that is in you, as you. That's it. They are not going to "give" you peace or enlightenment; they cannot. They will just tell you that you have it already and help you to recognize it.

So this explains a little about both the Guru outside and the one within. And, ultimately, know that they are one and the same.

CHAPTER 11

An Inner Commitment

Is it true that the disciple and Guru remain faithful to each other throughout eternity? If so, how do I know who my Guru is? And how can I choose a Guru in this life if I have already made a commitment in another?

Actually, there cannot be such an eternal commitment as you are talking about. Commitment can only be with a physical person—not between the Guru and disciple, because what is the Guru after all? The real Guru is the Spirit within you, the Awareness. It is your own Consciousness. The Consciousness in you, in me, in everybody is the same. It is a part of the Cosmic Consciousness. It is the God in you that is always watching you. It can guide you and tell you whether you are doing right or wrong.

But sometimes we are weak and don't listen to that. So you have an outside Guru who has realized the inner Truth and who faithfully follows this inner guide. That external Guru helps you know what is right and what is wrong until you no longer have doubts as to which inner voice to listen to. Your ego says, "Go ahead and do it." The intuition or inner guide says, "No, that's not the right thing to do."

But you don't know which is the ego and which is the inner knowing. Until you get that doubt cleared, you can go to a person who always follows their inner knowing and say, "This is what I feel: one voice says 'do,' one says 'don't.' I don't know what to do." So until you begin to follow your inner light, they help you.

Even while helping you, they will gradually teach you how to recognize and follow the inner Guru. They will never make you dependent on them. A Guru is there to liberate you, not to make you dependent on them.

I said there is no eternal commitment with the Guru as a physical person, but you are eternally committed to their Consciousness which is not different from your own Consciousness.

It's something like you want to clean your face but you don't know exactly where the dirt is. What will you do? You will stand in front of a mirror, see the dirt, wash your face and go away. So the Guru acts like that mirror. You go in front of them and they tell you, "There is that mistake; correct it." You correct it and go away. If you keep yourself clean you don't need a mirror after a while. That should be the way a Guru functions. They will never enslave you.

If anybody ever says, "You are eternally committed to me. You cannot go out or do this or that," then know that they are not a true Guru. No Guru will ever bind you. They will give you your freedom. They will only instruct you. If you are not ready to follow, they will wait. They have no business to curse or condemn you.

In fact no Guru will label themselves as a Guru. They feel they are always still learning. You call them a Guru because you see something good in them which you wish to learn, and they behave like a Guru because you want it that way. A president does not become the president by themselves. All the people jointly vote to make them president.

Then they have to behave like a president, at least for the four-year period. It is the same with the Guru. By your own feeling, you make them a Guru and give them that duty: "Come on, teach me; do this for me." Then they should do it. But the minute you say, "Well, I don't want to be trained by you anymore," they are your Guru no longer.

If you don't feel that communication with one person, if you don't see your face clearly in one mirror, go to another one. That's all. There's nothing wrong in it. If I cannot help you I won't hesitate to say, "Go to somebody else," because I'm interested in your welfare. Like a doctor, if they can't cure you, should they say not to go to somebody else?

If I'm a good doctor and I'm interested in your welfare, I should clearly say, "Sorry, I can't diagnose your case," or "I don't have the proper remedy. But my good friend is an expert; go to them." I will even dial that friend and say, "I'm sending so-and-so to you. Please take care of them." Yes, that should be the attitude of a Guru. So don't feel bad in changing.

But that doesn't mean you can keep on changing and benefit from that. Wait until you know the person well before you decide on them as your Guru. And when you do go to them, follow their practices well. Your own conscience should say you have followed it well. If after sincere practice you still don't get any benefit, then you can go to somebody else. But if you don't gain much due to your own lack of practice, you cannot blame the teacher and go to another person. That other person will also give you something similar and there again you won't do well. You will go to a third person. That means you will be digging shallow wells everywhere. You'll never get water anywhere.

When once you begin to dig in one place, keep digging and you will certainly get water. Otherwise you're wasting your time. All the true Gurus are interested in your welfare. And fundamentally all their teachings are the same, though superficially their methods may differ. The superficial differences don't matter much. It's something like whatever you eat will appease your hunger; any nutritious food will satisfy your hunger if you are really hungry.

CHAPTER 12
When a Guru or Disciple Dies

What becomes of the relationship of the Guru and disciple when the disciple dies? What if the Guru dies first?

Well, death means discarding the physical body. Your spiritual practices are not done by the body or recorded by the body alone, they are all in the mind—in the mental or astral body.

When the physical body dies, the astral body still has all those impressions. If your Guru is still alive you will still receive their blessings, follow their directions and communicate with them in the astral level. Even here at this lecture there may be many disembodied souls around. They come without any registration, without giving any donation!

If a disciple's destiny brings them another body and allows them to remember the Guru, they will come back to that Guru. But if they were not a very serious student, once they get a new body, those impressions will sink down in the mind, while only the predominant desires in the astral body will come to the surface. According to those predominant desires, they will lead their life. When those desires are exhausted, then the old submerged desires might come to the surface.

If those desires happen to be the ones that were built up while the person was with the Guru, they will come in search of that Guru. The continuity of the relationship is not broken because our desires and our thoughts never die.

On the other hand, if the Guru dies, they will continue to guide their students from the astral level. If the Guru desires to come into another body and continue to serve, then they will come again in another body.

In "Guru" there are no differences, it's only the bodies that are different. The realization is the same. The disciple will get another realized person as their Guru—or in other words, the Guru in a different body. So there is a continuity because the Guru-disciple relationship is based on the Truth. That's why many times when you meet your

Guru for the first time you feel you have known them for ages, but your memories are not vivid because of the change in the bodies. If your mind is really clear you can even have vivid memories of that also.

Closing Message

If you really surrender and give yourself totally, your Guru will swallow you up one day. You will lose your sense of separateness and thus they will make you a Guru. What happens to a drop of water when it falls into the sea? It loses its name "drop," and the form of drop, but it becomes the sea. You see?

Let us know that in Truth we are the Divine Image, the image of God. Somehow the veil of our ego prevents us from realizing this. Just remove that veil. It is that veil that is the basis for all these mental dramas. It creates all kinds of problems, troubles, anxieties and fears.

So please, if anybody has that self-centered or selfish ego, say, "E-go." Don't welcome any selfishness anymore. Once that goes away you become humble and your mind will be totally under your control. You will become the master.

I'm not going to stipulate certain practices to achieve this, do anything you want. But see that your mind remains in that tranquility, that purity, that neutrality. No Guru can ever take some Light and put it into you or bring God to you. And there's no need for them to do that because you have it already. If you were to get it from them you might lose it one day. Instead, you have it—know you are that. The Guru only helps you know it.

You fail to notice that Light because of the unclean or selfish ego and the mental disturbances it causes. So purify the mind; control the mind. Or, first control the body and the *prana* [life force] and when they are calmed, the mind will be calmed automatically. Then nothing can hide the Truth from you. If you are that pure, you are blessed. Then the God in you shines out. You know that you are God and others know that you are God.

So may that great Guru, the omnipresent Guru who is everywhere, shine from all angles by your refinement. May that Guru express through your own purity, humility, charity and generosity so the whole world could enjoy peace through you. That is my sincere wish and prayer. *Om Shanti*

About the Author
Sri Swami Satchidananda

Sri Swami Satchidananda was one of the great Yoga masters to bring the classical Yoga tradition to the Western world in the 1960s. He taught Yoga postures and meditation, and he introduced students to a vegetarian diet and a more compassionate lifestyle. The distinctive teachings that he brought with him blend the classical path of Yoga, the nondual philosophy of India and the interfaith ideals he pioneered.

These concepts and practices influenced a generation and spawned a Yoga culture that is flourishing today. Currently, over 35 million Americans (and 300 million worldwide) practice Yoga as a means for managing stress, promoting health, slowing down the aging process, and creating a more meaningful life.

The Integral Yoga® teachings of Swami Satchidananda are a pathway to an "easeful body, peaceful mind, and a useful life," as he said, and to harmony, balance, integration, and Self-Realization. The Integral Yoga method is a synthesis of six classical branches of Yoga: Hatha, Raja, Japa, Karma, Bhakti, and Jnana. Its aim is to purify and calm the body and mind in order to experience the peace and joy that is our true nature.

Integral Yoga practitioners bring that peace into the world by fostering interfaith harmony and leading service-oriented lives. Founded in 1966, there are currently 30 Integral Yoga centers on six of the seven continents and over 20,000 certified Integral Yoga teachers and therapists worldwide.

Today, these centers, teachers and therapists offer classes, workshops, and retreats. They also offer Yoga teacher training featuring all aspects of Integral Yoga and a Yoga therapist training program. Many Integral Yoga teachers and therapists have become leaders in the changing paradigm of modern Yoga and healthcare, as well as founding successful programs for specific populations. Integral Yoga-inspired programs include Dr. Dean Ornish's landmark work in reversing heart disease, Dr. Michael Lerner's noted Commonweal Cancer Help program, Sonia Sumar's Yoga for the Special Child, and Rev. Jivana Heyman's Accessible Yoga, among many others.

In 1979, Swami Satchidananda was inspired to establish Satchidananda Ashram–Yogaville®. Founded on his teachings, it is a large residential community, with a programs and retreat center, and training academy for Yoga and Yoga therapy. Yogaville is a haven where people can study and practice the teachings of Swami Satchidananda and Integral Yoga. It is a multifaith community where people of various backgrounds can come together to realize their essential oneness.

One of the focal points of Yogaville is the Light Of Truth Universal Shrine (LOTUS). This unique interfaith shrine honors the Spirit that unites all the world religions, while it celebrates their diversity. People from all over the world come there to meditate and pray. On the occasion of his birth centennial in 2014, a second LOTUS was opened at Swami Satchidananda's birthplace in South India.

Swami Satchidananda served on the advisory boards of many Yoga, world peace, and interfaith organizations. Over the years, he received many honors for his humanitarian service, including the Juliet Hollister Award presented at the United Nations and in 2002, the U Thant Peace Award. In 2014, he was posthumously honored as an "interfaith visionary," when the James Parks Morton Interfaith Award was presented by the Interfaith Center of New York.

Swami Satchidananda is the author of numerous books, while his translation and commentary on *The Yoga Sutras of Patanjali*, the foundation of Yoga philosophy, is the best-selling book of its kind. He is also the subject of the documentary, *Living Yoga: The Life and Teachings of Swami Satchidananda*.

For more information:

swamisatchidananda.org
integralyoga.org